For Oscar G – M.B
For Sarah Limo – A.M

BLOOMSBURY CHILDREN'S BOOKS
Bloomsbury Publishing Plc
50 Bedford Square, London, WC1B 3DP, UK
29 Earlsfort Terrace, Dublin 2, Ireland

BLOOMSBURY, BLOOMSBURY CHILDREN'S BOOKS and the Diana logo are trademarks of Bloomsbury Publishing Plc

First published in Great Britain 2023 by Bloomsbury Publishing Plc

A catalogue record for this book is available from the British Library

ISBN: HB: 978-1-5266-4707-8; PB: 978-1-5266-4706-1; eBook: 978-1-5266-6168-5
2 4 6 8 10 9 7 5 3 1

FSC
www.fsc.org

MIX
Paper from
responsible sources
FSC® C020056

Printed and bound in China by Leo Paper Products, Heshan, Guangdong

Moira Butterfield

Adam Ming

DOES A MONKEY GET GRUMPY?

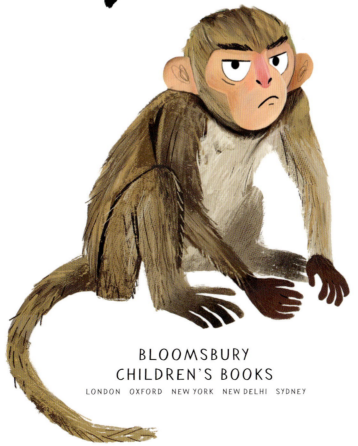

BLOOMSBURY
CHILDREN'S BOOKS

LONDON OXFORD NEW YORK NEW DELHI SYDNEY

Humans have all sorts of feelings ...

sad

excited

lonely

happy

grumpy

loving

playful

scared

We show our feelings in our faces, in how we move and what we say.

Animals feel things as well
but – though they **hoot** or **bark** or **squawk** –
unlike humans, they can't talk.

I can't speak. I squeak,
squeak, squeak!

We share our world with animals and so it's
good for me and you to understand their feelings, too.
Let's start by watching what they do ...

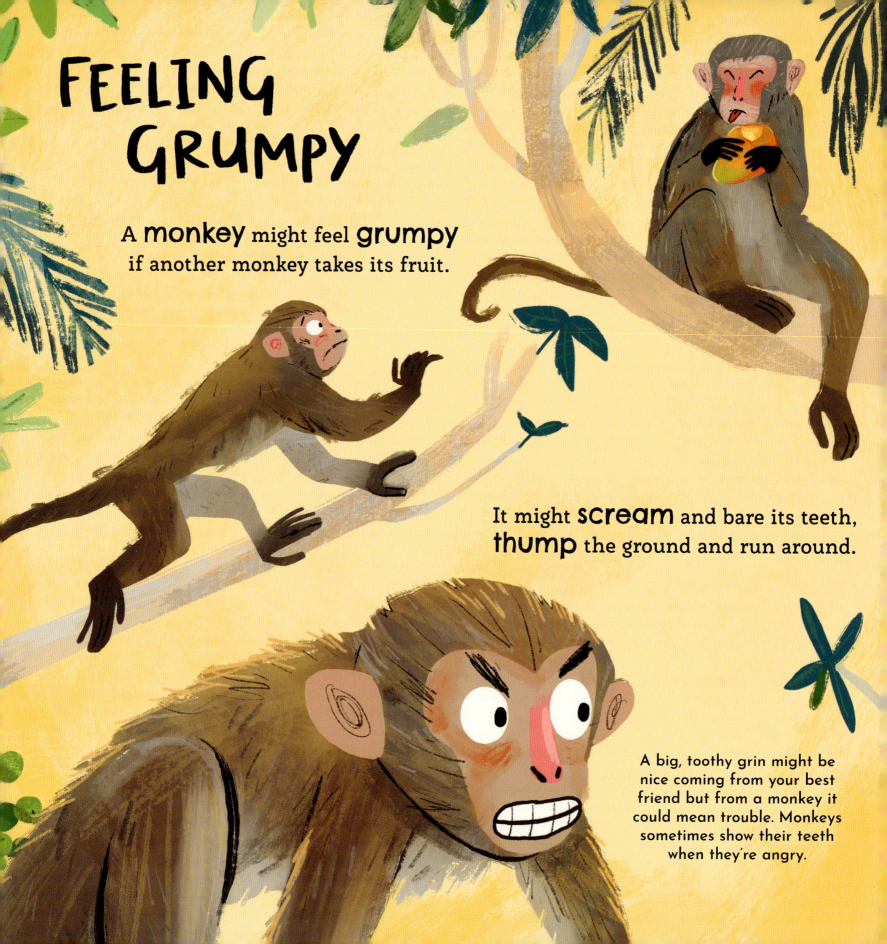

FEELING GRUMPY

A **monkey** might feel **grumpy** if another monkey takes its fruit.

It might **scream** and bare its teeth, **thump** the ground and run around.

A big, toothy grin might be nice coming from your best friend but from a monkey it could mean trouble. Monkeys sometimes show their teeth when they're angry.

Friends help to **calm** the monkey down
by picking fleas from off its fur.
They make their **peace** and get to eat
a juicy little jungle treat.

Yummy fleas!
Yes please.

Monkeys brush
and clean each other's
fur after getting angry,
just like you might hug
someone to make up
after falling out.

FEELING HAPPY

A **horse** will feel especially **happy** with some friends it really likes.

When horses meet to say **hello**, their happy feelings really show!

Happy horses nuzzle and gently rub each other's necks and faces.

I FEEL HAPPY, TOO

When they're playing, **rats** will squeak.
They make a happy **cheep, cheep, cheep.**

Playtime is cheeping time!

Pet rats often squeak when they're happy, just like you might laugh when you're tickled! This noise is too high-pitched for us humans to hear though.

FEELING SAD

A **Canada goose** will raise its chicks with the same partner every year.

But if it finds its partner dead, it bows its head, swims off **alone** and drifts around all on its **own**.

I miss my partner. Honk, honk.

If its partner dies, a goose will leave its flock for a while. It sometimes makes sad honking noises, just like you might cry out when you're upset.

Returning to friends back in its flock
should help cure its **heartbreak** pain.
And it may, one happy day,
find itself new **love** again!

Wolves, elephants, whales and
parrots all show they're sad
if their friends die, but only
humans shed tears of sadness
when they are upset.

FEELING EXCITED

A dog who's **excited** will show how it feels by **wag-wag-wagging** its tail super-fast. It's thinking ...

Wow! I just can't wait. That tasty treat is going to be GREAT!

An excited dog might also bow down and make happy yapping sounds, especially when it's time to play.

I FEEL EXCITED, TOO

Yippee!

When **COWS** go out to fresh new fields
after a winter in their barn,
they get so **excited** they **skip** and **prance**.
It looks as if they do a **dance**.

In Denmark, people come
to watch cows leaving their
barns for grassy fields
after winter. It's called
Dancing Cows Day.

When **guinea pigs** get **excited**,
they might start bouncing ...

... pop, pop, **pop** ...

Like popcorn pinging in a pan!

When a guinea pig jumps for
joy it's called 'popcorning'.
Chinchillas do it too.

FEELING SCARED

If something scares a **frilled lizard**, it opens its yellow mouth and **hisses**, then **flares** out its orange ruff ...

Don't mess with me! I'm BIG and TOUGH!

The lizard tries to look as scary as possible, telling its enemy to GO AWAY! Lots of animals use this trick when they are scared, just like you might shout for help when you're in danger.

What if the **tough-guy** act's not working?
OK, lizard. Time to **flee**!
Run, run, quickly
up that tree!

Yikes!

Frilled lizards live in Australia.
Their enemies include hungry snakes,
wild cats and big birds of prey.

Deciding whether to fight
or run away is called 'fight
or flight'. We all get fight or
flight feelings when we are
threatened with danger.

FEELING PLAYFUL

Wild dolphins like to **play** a game of **catching seaweed** underwater.

Your turn!

They find a handy seaweed strand and **flip** it as it **floats** around, trying to stop it **sinking down.**

Playing a turn-taking game is great practise for dolphins, who hunt fish together as a team.

I FEEL PLAYFUL, TOO

Octopuses kept in tanks will play with rubber balls and toys.

Playtime!

An octopus has nine brains! There's one big one in its head and a mini one in each arm. No wonder it's clever enough to play these smart games!

They'll make the balls pop UP and down and have fun blowing toys around.

FEELING LONELY

If a **rabbit** lives alone,
it might feel **lonely** on its own.
It could get **sick** or leave its food,
without some **fun** to lift its mood.

I wish someone would come and play with me.

In the wild, rabbits are social animals, which means they live in a group. That's why pet rabbits are happier with company. Guinea pigs like company, too.

The rabbit's **loneliness** is sure to end
if it gets a **furry friend**.
Rabbits usually feel better
when they spend some time **together**.

I feel better with
you around.

You can also help a rabbit feel
less lonely by playing with it and
letting it run around. Rabbits can
live happily with other animals
too, such as chickens, but they
like to be with other rabbits best.

FEELING SHY

Wild animals are often shy because they're very scared of danger.

Getting close will make them stressed. Watching from afar is best.

Many wild creatures are hunted by other animals, so they must stay on their guard, ready to run. They are shy because they don't trust other animals not to attack.

Deer appear at **quiet** times.
Their nostrils flare to **smell** the air ...
They listen out for any **sound** ...
An **enemy** might be around!

A deer's sense of smell is much better than a human's. Strange smells tell them danger is near.

I hope nobody can see me.

Deer spend a lot of time hiding, but come out to feed in the early morning or the evening. The dim light makes them harder to spot.

FEELING LOVE

When two **mute** **swans** become a pair
they do a special kind of **dance**.
Their beaks **gently touch** as they glide
and move their necks from side to side.

Will you be mine?

Swans dance to attract a partner.
During this dance, they sometimes ruffle
up their feathers and bow to each other.
It's an important moment because this
partnership will last for life.

The dancing swans will soon go on
to build a **nest** and hatch some **eggs**.
Every year, forever and ever,
living their feathery lives **together**.

I'm glad I chose you.

In the animal kingdom, it's very
unusual to show lifelong love for
friends and family. However, monkeys,
elephants, whales and apes also do
this. And humans, of course!

FEELING

There, there.

Elephants are very caring and will **COMFORT** upset friends.

They touch them with a **gentle** trunk and stand beside them for a while. It's like **hugging**, but elephant style.

An elephant will also make low rumbling noises to show it cares. It's saying: 'I know you are upset. I understand and I'm here for you.' Just like you might say to your friend!

KIND

Elephants who've **hurt** themselves
are tended by their **kindly** friends.
A helping trunk is always there
as a way to show they care!

I'm here,
my friend.

A kind elephant called Chana
became famous for helping
her blind friend Ploy Thong.
She would lead her around at
the elephant rescue centre,
helping her find food.

So now we know by **watching** them,
that animals have feelings, too,
just like me and **you**!

Furry, scaly, short or tall.

Squeaky, beaky, big or small ...

Let's show **kindness** to them all!